1/19

HOW TO LIVE LIKE

A CARIBBEAN
PIRATE

contents

Pirate!

It's the year 1717, and you're in the city of Charleston in the North Carolina colony. My name is Jamie Flynn. There's a forest of ships tied up against the pier. Some ships have slaves from Africa. Others are headed back to Europe.

But who are those shifty-looking men over there? *Uh-oh!* They've spotted me listening. They're coming this way! *Agh*, too late! Before I can struggle, they've put a sack over my head, and thrown me into a rowboat. "Sharp eyes, eh? He's just what we need for a lookout!" Then it all goes black. I've been kidnapped by pirates!

Golden Age of Piracy

Between 1716 and 1726, pirate ships roamed the seas near America and into the Caribbean. Many a lone ship caught sight of a pirate ship racing toward them over the waves and knew they were doomed. Historians now call it the Golden Age of Piracy. But for the victims of pirates it was anything but golden! Pirate leaders such as Black Bart, Black Sam Bellamy, and Calico Jack were ruthless cutthroats, and you didn't want to be on a ship attacked by one of them!

Florida

Gulf of Mexico

Cuba

Dominican Republic

Caribbean Sea

WARNING!

If you live in a seaport, you'd better watch out for "press gangs"—ruthless gangs that recruit pirates by force!

A Pirate Ship

Oh no! It seems I've been taken aboard the most fearsome of all pirate ships, the *Queen Anne's Revenge*, flagship of the terrifying pirate Blackbeard.

Like nearly all pirate ships, *Queen Anne's Revenge* is a stolen ship. To make it fast and dangerous, the pirates stripped away its cumbersome "castles," the deck structures at front and back. Then they knocked through the lower decks to open it up so it could take lots of extra men. And they cut holes in the hull to poke forty cannons through. That makes it a formidable ship for fast attack! Unarmed ships better watch out!

Blackbeard's Ship

In 1996, divers found a wreck lying in 28 feet (8.5 meters) of water just off Atlantic Beach in North Carolina. In 2011, the National Geographic Society confirmed that this was *Queen Anne's Revenge*, run aground in 1718, complete with a cannon. Among the thousands of items found was a medical syringe showing that Blackbeard did look after his crew!

North Carolina

Altantic Ocean

A cutaway of the
Queen Anne's Revenge

Beached!

It's hard to keep a pirate ship in tip-top condition, because we can't go into any regular port for maintenance. We have to steal all the equipment we need from the ships we attack. And every now and then, we need to run the ship aground to scrape the hull clean of barnacles and weeds that might slow us down. That's seriously hard work!

Life on Board

"UP THE MAST, BOY! NOW!" That's the mate yelling! Because I'm small and light, and have sharp eyes, I'm the lookout in the crow's nest—the most dangerous part of the ship! It's the tiny bucket right up at the top of the main mast, swaying more than 50 feet (15 m) above the deck.

I often have to climb up slippery, wet rigging as gales are howling and waves crash over the ship. It's really, really frightening when the ship rolls over, the mast leans and I'm left hanging high out over the crashing waves. I feel sick most of the time! The last lookout before me crashed to his death on the deck when his foot got caught by a stray sail line. But I can see a long way from up here—and if I'm the first to see a ship for us to attack, I'll get a reward of one gold piece!

Some of our crew were kidnapped like me, but many chose to come. Life is tough on other ships and on land, too, now. Being a pirate is dangerous, but you've got the freedom of the sea.

Below Decks

Life on a pirate ship is no fun at all! The food's just stale biscuits and, if I'm lucky, a bit of salt beef so tough it'd be easier to eat my shoes (if I had any!). And there are no beds—just hammocks for the senior crew. Lookout boys like me just curl up on ropes or sacking below deck. It's really cold and wet and dark, and the smell is terrible. *Ugh!* AND there are RATS!

Blackbeard!

Oh no! I'm being hauled up before the captain, the monstrous Blackbeard. His real name is Edward Teach, and he probably came from a decent British family. But he's called Blackbeard because of his huge black beard. It's no ordinary beard, I can tell you! It's huge and dark and knotted into plaits that look like writhing snakes. And when he goes into battle, he often ties lighted fireworks into them to make himself look super scary! And now he's shouting at me like an angry bear!

They say Blackbeard is so strong he can cut a man in half with a single blow from his cutlass. And he's so nasty, he shot his own mate in the knees just for a laugh! But maybe he spreads these rumors himself. If his victims believe he's so dreadful, they'll give up without a fight when they hear Blackbeard is coming. . . I'm sure he just winked at me!

Kinds of Pirates

The "buccaneers" of the 1600s were pirates given "letters of marque" by the French and British so they could legally raid Spanish enemy ships. A "buccan" was the beach barbeque they liked. "Privateers" were private ships hired by governments to attack enemies. "Corsairs" were what the English called French pirates, and what the French called Muslim pirates. "Barbary pirates" were Muslim pirates from the Barbary Coast of North Africa.

Here are some other scary pirates:

Captain Kidd: Hanged 1701, London. Best prize: the *Quedagh Merchant*'s silks and gold

Black Bart Roberts: Killed 1722, off Nigeria in Africa. Best prize: fifteen ships in three days!

Henry Morgan: Died 1688, Jamaica. Best prize: Destroying the Spanish fleet in Venezuela

Sam Bellamy: Died 1717, in a storm. Best prize: *Whydah*'s indigo, gold, and silver

Calico Jack Rackham: Hanged 1720, Jamaica. Crew included two women captured with him (right)

Anne Bonny and Mary Read: Escaped hanging because they were pregnant. Read died 1721. Bonny's end is uncertain.

Booty Haul

Once we capture our prize ship, it's time to divide the spoils. Of course, Blackbeard takes the lion's share, but we pirates like to divide our booty. Gold and jewels are nice. But most ships don't carry them. What we usually get is food, cloth, tools, and weapons, which are far more useful to us. You can't eat gold when you're hungry! And you can't buy weapons out at sea. Sugar, wine, and tobacco are always nice treats after months living on stale beer and dry salty biscuits.

Buried Treasure Myth

Robert Louis Stevenson's famous story *Treasure Island* gave people the idea that pirates often buried their stolen treasure, and then left maps with clues about where to find it. But only one pirate is known to have buried treasure—William Kidd. He hid his loot in 1701 when he thought he was going to be arrested. But he didn't leave a map. . .

Pieces of Eight

A piece of eight was a Spanish silver coin. Pirates rarely saw them. But people often link them with pirates because in *Treasure Island*, Long John Silver's parrot keeps repeating "pieces of eight!"

Dressed Like a Pirate!

My own clothes wore out long ago. So I've got a new suit of pirate garb. We pirates have our own way of dressing. It's a mix of items stolen from our victims—and ones made from the rolls of luxurious cloth we rescued from a ship. Just like many of my fellows, my jacket's way too big for me, and my pantaloons are baggy and colorful. But I look every inch a pirate.

Phrase Book

Pirates have their own way of talking...

Shiver me timbers! Expressing a nasty shock, based on the way the timbers (masts) shiver (shake) when hit by a cannonball

Avast ye! Stop (you)!

Anchors aweigh! Lift the anchor just clear of the bottom

Landlubber! The worst insult to a pirate. A lubber is someone clumsy, and who is happiest living ashore.

Strike colors Lower the flag and surrender

Swabbie A swab is a kind of mop, and a swabbie is the poor idiot who has to scrub all the blood off the decks after a fight. *Ugh!* That's me after I ran into the first mate by accident...

Three-cornered Hat!

My proudest possession is my three-cornered or tricorne hat. Ordinary crew aren't allowed to wear them, but I'm Blackbeard's boy, now, so I've got one. Tricornes don't just look good. The broad brim keeps the ocean spray off your face, and the turn-up acts like a gutter.

That's Your Lot

In November 1718, we were partying on Ocracoke Island off the Carolina coast when we saw two ships flying navy colors heading our way. With the tide out, they couldn't reach us over the sandbar that night. Next morning, as the tide rose and navy ships raced in over the bar, Blackbeard calmly steered his ship toward the beach. He must have gone mad! But then he steered us through a tiny gap between the beach and a sandbar. The navy ships slammed into the bar and stuck. *Aha!* But as our ship fired its cannon at them, it lurched back and soon we were stuck, too.

It looked like all the navy sailors had been killed by our cannon, so we rowed across and boarded their ship. Oh no, it was a trap. They were faking! The navy captain, Maynard, met Blackbeard face-to-face. They both fired pistols. But as Blackbeard swung his sword for the final blow, another sailor cut his throat from behind. That was the end of Blackbeard—and my life as a pirate! Hooray!

Many pirates who were caught alive were taken to London, tried, and then hanged—including Captain Kidd. The rope broke when they tried to hang Kidd, so they had to hang him a second time.

Ten Peculiar Pirate Facts

1 There were around two thousand pirates in the Caribbean in 1717.

2 Pirates compensated men who were injured in battle. For example, a man who lost his right arm would receive six hundred pieces of eight or six slaves.

3 If someone betrayed a pirate crew, they were sent an ace of spades playing card. This meant they were going to be killed. . .

4 Some pirates really did have wooden legs. They often fought, and anyone badly wounded in the leg might need to have it cut off—to stop the gangrene (infection) from spreading and killing him.

5 Pirates caught parrots in South America and taught them to talk. But they usually sold the parrots later for a high price.

6 When Dutch pirate Dirk Chivers captured naval captain Sawbridge, the prisoner complained so much that Chivers sewed up his mouth with a needle and thread.

7 In 1825, when pirates captured the ship *Eliza Ann*, they killed the crew. But they spared a woman—Lucretia Parker—who lived to tell the tale.

8 Pirates liked to give their ships scary names. Benito de Soto called his the *Black Joke*. And Danish pirate John Derdrake's vessel had the ominous name *Sudden Death*.

9 It was not uncommon for pirates to kidnap boys. Some boys, called "powder monkeys," had to keep the cannons topped up with gunpowder. Their life was very tough indeed!

10 When Blackbeard was killed, his killers cut off Blackbeard's head and tossed his body over the side. It was said that his headless body still swam around, yelling, "Where's my head?"

Glossary

belaying pin:

a solid metal or wooden handle used to secure rigging—and a handy weapon

buccaneers:

pirates legalized by the British and French with "letters of marque" to attack Spanish ships

buckler:

a small, round shield that can be used as an offensive weapon

cutlass:

shortish, heavy hacking sword with one cutting edge; easy to wield

flintlock:

a pistol fired by striking a flint against metal to create the spark that sets fire to the powder

keelhauling:

dragging someone under the bottom of the boat for punishment

marooning:

leaving someone stranded on a desert island for punishment

tricorne:

a three-cornered hat popular with pirates

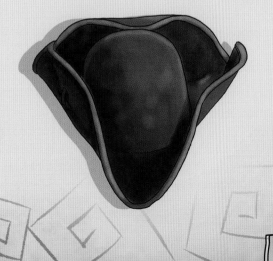

INDEX

The Author

John Farndon is Royal Literary Fellow at Anglia Ruskin University in Cambridge, United Kingdom, and the author of a huge number of books for adults and children on science and nature. He has been shortlisted four times for the Royal Society's Young People's Book Prize.

The Artist

Tatio Viana lives in Madrid, Spain, and worked as an art director before turning to what he really loves: illustrating. Entirely self-taught, he creates his artwork digitally, but dreams of illustrating his own stories with paints and crayons—especially for his son, Elías, to read.